Deserts

by Susan H. Gray

Content Adviser: Terrence E. Young Jr., M.Ed., M.L.S.,
Jefferson Parish (La.) Public Schools

Reading Adviser: Dr. Linda D. Labbo, Department of Reading
Education, College of Education,
The University of Georgia

COMPASS POINT BOOKS

Minneapolis, Minnesota

Compass Point Books
3722 West 50th Street, #115
Minneapolis, MN 55410

Visit Compass Point Books on the Internet at *www.compasspointbooks.com* or e-mail your request
to *custserv@compasspointbooks.com*

Photographs ©: International Stock/Wayne Aldridge, cover; Index Stock Imagery, 4; Visuals Unlimited/Gerald and Buff
Corsi, 5; Photo Network/Henry T. Kaiser, 6; VCG/FPG International, 7; James P. Rowan, 8; Root Resources/James Blank, 9;
Index Stock Imagery/Jack Hoehn, Jr., 10; James P. Rowan, 11; Visuals Unlimited/Charles W. McRae, 13; Visuals
Unlimited/Francis E. Caldwell, 14; Visuals Unlimited/Link, 15; Chris Hellier/Corbis, 16; Photri-Microstock, 17, 18; Dave
Watts/Tom Stack and Associates, 19; Marco Corsetti/FPG International, 20; Ed Darack/Cole photo, 21; Visuals Unlimited/Arthur
Morris, 22; Photo Network/Esbin-Anderson, 23; Visuals Unlimited/Doug Sokell, 24; Cheryl A. Ertelt, 25; Visuals
Unlimited/Glenn Oliver, 26; Visuals Unlimited/John D. Cunningham, 27; Ron Thomas/FPG International, 28; James P. Rowan,
29; Jessie M. Harris, 30; Photri-Microstock, 31; Visuals Unlimited/Walt Anderson, 32; Visuals Unlimited/Gil Lopez-Espina, 33;
Visuals Unlimited/Rob and Ann Simpson, 34; Photri-Microstock/Humerford, 35; Root Resources/A.B. Sheldon, 36; Joe
McDonald/Tom Stack and Associates, 37; Cheryl A. Ertelt, 38; Visuals Unlimited/Joe McDonald, 39; Visuals Unlimited/Charles
W. McRae, 40; Visuals Unlimited/Rudolf Arndt, 41; Unicorn Stock Photos/Tommy Dodson, 42; Photri-Microstock, 43.

Editors: E. Russell Primm and Emily J. Dolbear
Photo Researcher: Svetlana Zhurkina
Photo Selector: Dawn Friedman
Design: Bradfordesign, Inc.

Library of Congress Cataloging-in-Publication Data
Gray, Susan Heinrichs.
   Deserts / by Susan H. Gray.
     p. cm. — (First reports)
   Includes bibliographical references (p.   ) and index.
   Summary: Describes some of the main deserts around the world, how deserts are formed,
and some of the plants and animals found in these dry areas.
    ISBN 0-7565-0019-2 (hardcover : lib. bdg.)
     1. Desert ecology—Juvenile literature. 2. Deserts—Juvenile literature. [1. Deserts. 2. Desert
ecology. 3. Ecology.] I. Title. II. Series.
   QH541.5.D4 G73 2000
   577.54—dc21   00-008529

Table of Contents

What Do You Think of Deserts?

People usually think of deserts as sandy, dry, lifeless, and blazing hot—and no wonder! Deserts have places with names such as Death Valley, Badwater Basin, and Funeral Peak. Some deserts go without

▲ *The Badwater Basin in Death Valley National Park, California*

rain for years. Some have hot, dry winds that sweep over miles of sand. But this picture of deserts is only partly true.

Deserts have two things in common. They get less than 10 inches (25 centimeters) of rain a year. And, in deserts, water rises into the air as a gas, or **evaporates**, very quickly.

▲ *A flash flood in the desert*

When it does rain in the desert, it rains for days at a time. Then there is a long dry period. Rain has powerful effects on desert lands. It washes away soil and carves deep canyons.

▲ *Rain and wind created the craggy surface of Death Valley*

Wind shapes the desert landscape too. It blows sand into high mounds called **dunes**. After a dune is formed, the wind still works on it. Wind sweeps up sand on one side of the dune and sand falls down the other side. Because of this, dunes shift. In very windy deserts, they can move up to 100 feet (30 meters) in a year!

▲ *Sand dunes in Namibia, Africa*

The desert ground is not all sandy. In some places, it is covered by rocks or gravel.

▲ *An organ pipe cactus growing in the rocky soil of the Sonoran Desert in Arizona*

Why Are Deserts Dry?

Mountains are the main reason deserts are so dry. Tall mountain ranges block rain clouds from passing. All

▲ *The Sierra Mountains of California*

▲ *Mt. Baker in the North Cascade Mountains, Washington*

the rain falls on one side of the mountain range.
The other side of the mountain range stays dry.
This is where deserts are found.

In North America, the Sierra Nevada and the Cascade Range block clouds. They stop the rain before it reaches the Great Basin Desert.

▲ *Arches National Park in the Great Basin Desert, Utah*

An average of about 6 to 12 inches (150 to 300 millimeters) of rain falls each year here. This is just enough to support life. This desert has an interesting drainage system. The water that runs off the land does not flow toward the sea. The water instead flows into basins. The lowest of these basins is the Great Salt Lake in Utah.

Are All Deserts Hot?

All deserts are dry. But not all deserts are hot. Wind blowing over cold water becomes cold. When cold, dry wind reaches land, it makes the land cold and dry too.

▲ *The Patagonian Desert in Argentina is cool and dry*

The Namib Desert in southwest Africa is right next to the Atlantic Ocean. Very cold water runs north along its coast. Winds blowing over this water become cold and dry. They blow right into the desert, keeping it cold and dry as well. Other cold deserts include the Great Basin in the United States and the Patagonian Desert in South America.

▲ *Mountains bordering the Namib Desert in Africa, the oldest desert in the world*

Even the hottest deserts can become icy cold at night though. Death Valley is in the Mojave Desert in California. In 1913, it had the highest temperature ever recorded in the United States. It got up to 134° Fahrenheit (57° Celsius). But when night falls in the Mojave, the temperature may drop to freezing.

▲ *Sunset over the Mojave Desert*

Deserts of the World

Deserts are found along two imaginary lines around the Earth. These lines are called the Tropic of Cancer and the Tropic of Capricorn. The deserts of North America, northern Africa, and Asia lie along the Tropic of Cancer. The deserts of South America, Australia, and southern Africa lie along the Tropic of Capricorn.

▲ A sign announcing the Tropic of Capricorn in Madagascar

The world's largest desert is the Sahara in Africa. It is almost as big as the United States. It gets less than 5 inches (13 centimeters) of rain in a year. In some areas, rain may not fall for years. Much of the Sahara is flat and sandy. But the center of the Sahara has high mountains covered with snow.

▲ *The Sahara Desert in Algeria, northern Africa*

The Thar Desert, also called the Indian Desert, is in India. People bring water through pipes or ditches to **irrigate** part of it. The irrigated area is used for farmland.

▲ *A shepherd with his flock in the irrigated desert of India*

Deserts cover much of the center of Australia. One of them, the Simpson Desert, has long rows of sand dunes running north to south. Southern Africa has the Kalahari Desert. Miners have been digging up

▲ *Flowers cover sand dunes after a rain in the Simpson Desert, Australia*

The Atacama Desert, Chile

diamonds there for years.

The Atacama Desert in the Northern part of Chile in South America is perhaps the driest place on Earth. One spot there had less than 1 inch (2.5 centimeters) of rain in forty-three years. This desert is bounded on the east by the Andes Mountains and on the west by the Pacific Ocean

North America has four deserts. They are the Great Basin, the Mojave, the Sonoran, and the Chihuahuan Deserts. They are all in the western

▲ *The Mojave Desert*

United States. The Great Basin reaches into Oregon and Washington. It is the only cool desert in North America. Southern parts of the Great Basin are much warmer, however.

▼ *The Sonoran Desert*

Desert Plants

▲ *Prickly pear cactus surrounded by desert verbena*

All plants and animals need water to live and grow. Plants and animals in the desert are able to live on very little water. They have special features that help them live in the desert.

Desert plants have roots, stems, and seeds that are just right for life in the desert. For example, the mesquite is a small tree found in North American deserts. It has one main root that grows straight down into the soil to reach moisture. This main root is called a taproot. Researchers have found mesquites with taproots more than 120 feet (37 meters) long!

▲ A velvet mesquite tree

◄ *A saguaro cactus*

Other desert plants have shallow root systems. The giant saguaro cactus of the Sonoran Desert has a huge network of roots. Its roots can spread as wide as 65 feet (20 meters). They lie right below the surface and quickly soak up any rain that falls.

The saguaro is interesting in another way. Like some other cactus plants, the saguaro has a trunk and branches with many grooves. When rain falls, the trunk swells up and the grooves disappear. A tall, saguaro can store more than five tons of water!

◀ *The grooves in a saguaro cactus swell when it rains.*

Cactus plants have several ways of protecting their stored water. Some have stems covered in sharp spines. This keeps animals from eating them. The old man cactus has a coat of long, white hair. Its coat helps protect the cactus from animals and the sun's harsh rays.

◄ Spines cover a saguaro cactus.

▲ Barrel cactus and other plants in the desert

Desert plants called **ephemerals** spring up from the ground when it rains. Their seeds can survive long dry periods. When there is enough rain, the seeds sprout. The new plants grow rapidly. They form flowers and new seeds while the ground is still moist. Then the plants die, leaving seeds to wait for the next rainfall.

▲ *Spring wildflowers bloom after a rain in the Sonoran Desert.*

The Troublesome Tamarisk

▲ *Tamarisk trees*

Tamarisk trees grow in Texas and Mexico. People brought them to America from Asia in the 1850s. They knew tamarisks grew in very dry areas. They hoped the roots would keep desert soil from washing away during rains.

As it turned out, tamarisks could grow just about anywhere! Now they cover thousands of square miles of dry and wet areas and choke out other plants. Many people are working to get rid of these pesky trees.

Animal Life in the Desert

▲ *A desert kangaroo rat*

Desert animals, like desert plants, can survive long dry periods. Their bodies and behaviors are ready for desert life. Most desert animals are very small and need little water. Also, they can easily find shelter when the desert gets too hot or too dry.

Kangaroo rats and pocket mice live in North

American deserts. In the daytime, they **burrow** into the ground. Then they seal up the entrance with soil. In this way, they escape the heat and block out dry air. When it cools down at night, they break open the seal and come out to eat.

▲ A mound made by a rat or mouse in the Arizona desert

The African ground squirrel searches for food in the daytime. It keeps its back to the sun and raises its tail. The tail provides shade that keeps the squirrel from getting too hot.

▲ *An African ground squirrel*

▲ *A spadefoot toad*

People usually don't think of toads as desert animals, because they live near water. The spadefoot toad of the Sonoran Desert is different, however. It burrows as deep as 3 feet (90 centimeters) into the ground. It stays in its moist underground home for about nine months, waiting for rain. Finally, when the rain falls, the toad struggles up to the surface. Other spadefoot toads come out too. They mate and the females lay eggs. These hatch into tadpoles, which grow into young toads before the water dries up again.

Many kinds of **reptiles** live in deserts. Rattlesnakes called sidewinders and poisonous lizards called Gila

▲ *You can see the rattle on the tail of this sidewinder.*

monsters are among the reptiles that live in the American Southwest. The large, slow-moving Gila monster stores fat in its huge tail.

▲ A Gila monster

Horned toads and chuckwallas also are lizards of North American deserts. When it gets scared, a chuckwalla rushes into a crack in a nearby rock. It breathes in air and swells up. It becomes so tightly packed in the crack that nothing can pull it out.

▲ *A Texas horned toad*

A chuckwalla

One of the most unusual animals is a black beetle of the Namib Desert. When fog rolls in, this little beetle climbs to the top of a sand dune and faces the fog. Then it bows its head and raises up its back. Mist gathers on its back and drops of water roll down into its mouth. When it is satisfied, the beetle crawls back to its nest.

Desert birds have interesting ways of getting water. The elf owl of North America is the world's smallest owl. During the day, it lives in a hole in the saguaro cactus. It flies out at night to snatch up centipedes and scorpions for dinner. The elf owl gets its water from eating these living things.

▲ An elf owl

The sandgrouse is a bird that lives in the Namib Desert. Sometimes it nests miles away from water. Baby chicks get water from their father. He flies to distant ponds and wallows in the water. His feathers soak up the water like a sponge. When he returns to the nest, the chicks sip the water from his feathers.

▲ *A pair of sandgrouses at an African watering hole*

Camels of Asian and African deserts can go for many days without water. Then they have to stock up on water again. One thirsty camel was recorded gulping down 49 gallons (186 liters) of water in a day! Camels can lose more than one-fourth of the water in their bodies without becoming ill. This would kill most other large animals.

▲ *Camels in the desert*

Camels do not store water in their humps, as many people think. Instead, their humps store fat for use when food is hard to find. As the fat is changed into body fuel, it releases water.

Camels are well protected from the desert winds. Their long eyelashes protect their eyes, and their nostrils clamp shut to keep out sand.

▲ *A camel closes its nostrils to keep out sand.*

Clearly, the desert holds a lot more than hot, dry sand. Deserts are among the most interesting places in the world.

▲ *An oasis in the Sahara Desert, Africa*

Glossary

burrow—to dig a tunnel

dune—a high mound of sand piled up by the wind

ephemeral—a plant that grows, flowers, and dies in a few days

evaporation—the process by which water rises into the air as a gas

irrigate—to bring water to farmland through pipes or ditches

reptiles—horny-scaled animals unable to produce their own body heat

Did You Know?

- Camels can live as long as forty years.

- Sand covers only 10 to 20 percent of most deserts. The rest of the land is covered with gravel, rock, and dry lakebeds.

- Large groups of sand dunes are called dune fields. Very large groups of sand dunes are called sand seas.

- The Gobi Desert in China often gets severe blizzards in winter.

At a Glance

Location: Parts of Africa, Asia, Australia, North America, and South America

Amount of rain or snow each year: 8 inches (20 centimeters)

Description: Very dry

Common animals: Kangaroo rats, camels, snakes, lizards

Common plants: Sparse grasses, small shrubs, cactuses

Want to Know More?

At the Library

Fowler, Allan. *It Could Still Be a Desert*. Danbury, Conn.: Children's Press, 1997.

Morris, Neil. *Deserts*. New York: Crabtree Pub. Co., 1996.

Savage, Stephen. *Animals of the Desert*. Austin, Tex.: Raintree Steck-Vaughn, 1997.

Steiner, Barbara A. *Desert Trip*. San Francisco: Sierra Club Books for Children, 1996.

On the Web

The Desert Biome
http://lsb.syr.edu/projects/cyberzoo/biomes/desert.html
For information about geological events, weather, and animals associated with this type of region

Desert USA
http://www.desertusa.com/
For an introduction to North American deserts

Through the Mail

Desert Botanical Garden
1201 North Galvin Parkway
Phoenix, AZ 85008
To receive nature guides about the desert plants and birds

On the Road

Joshua Tree National Park
74485 National Park Drive
Twentynine Palms, CA 92277
760/367-5500
To visit where the Sonoran and Mojave Deserts meet

About the Author

Susan H. Gray holds bachelor's and master's degrees in zoology from the University of Arkansas in Fayetteville. She has taught classes in general biology, human anatomy, and physiology. She has also worked as a freshwater biologist and scientific illustrator. In her twenty years as a writer, Susan H. Gray has covered many topics and written a variety of science books for children.